The ReGender App

"This book is brilliant. ... The scene at the airport had me laughing out loud. ..." Katya, Goodreads

"Recommended to any book club and to people who are interested in gender differences and gender discrimination." Mesca Elin, Psychromatic Redemption

License to Do That

"I'm very much intrigued by the issues raised in this narrative. I also enjoy the author's voice, which is unapologetically combative but also funny and engaging." A.S.

"I love Froot Loup! You make me laugh out loud all the time!" Celeste M.

"A thought-provoking premise and a wonderful cast of characters." rejection letter from publisher

The Blasphemy Tour

"With plenty of humor and things to think about throughout, *The Blasphemy Tour* is a choice pick ..." *Midwest Book Review*

"Jass Richards has done it again. As I tell anyone who wants to listen, Jass is a comedy genius, she writes the funniest books and always writes the most believable unbelievable characters and scenes ... I knew this book was a winner when ... a K9 unit dog kind of eats their special brownies... and dances Thriller. ... Rev and Dylan are not your ordinary guy and girl protagonists with sexual tension and a romantic interest, at all. They both defy gender roles, and they are so smart and opinionated, it's both funny and made me think at the same time. ... They tour around the USA, in their lime green bus that says 'There are no gods. Deal with it.' Overall, I highly recommend anything by Jass, especially this one book, which is full of comedy gold and food for thought." May Arend, Brazilian Book Worm

"If I were Siskel and Ebert I would give this book Two Thumbs Way Up. ... Yes, it is blasphemy toward organized religion but it gives you tons of Bible verses to back up its premises. And besides, it's pure entertainment. There's a prequel which I recommend you read first. *The Road Trip Dialogues*. ... I only hope there will be a third book." L.K. Killian

The Road Trip Dialogues

"I am impressed by the range from stoned silliness to philosophical perspicuity, and I love your comic rhythm." L. S.

"This is engaging, warm, funny work, and I enjoyed what I read. ..." rejection letter from publisher

"Just thought I'd let you know I'm on the Fish'n'Chips scene and laughing my ass off." Ellie Burmeister

"These two need stable jobs. Oh wait, no. Then we wouldn't get any more road trips. Fantastic book which expands the mind in a laid back sort of way. Highly recommended." lindainalabama

Dogs Just Wanna Have Fun

"Funny and entertaining! I looked forward to picking up this book at the end of a long day." Mary Baluta

"...terrifically funny and ingeniously acerbic ..." Dr. Patricia Bloom, My Magic Dog

"...laugh-out-loud funny." M.W., Librarything

This Will Not Look Good on My Resume

"Ya made me snort root beer out my nose!" Moriah Jovan, *The Proviso*

"Darkly humorous." Jennifer Colt, The Hellraiser of the Hollywood Hills

"HYSTERICAL! ... There are really no words to describe how funny this book is. ... Really excellent book." Alison, Goodreads

"This book is like a roller coaster ride on a stream of consciousness. ... Altogether, a funny, quirky read ..." Grace Krispy, Motherlode; Book Reviews and Original Photography

"Brett has trouble holding down a job. Mainly because she's an outspoken misanthrope who is prone to turn a dead-end job into a social engineering experiment. Sometimes with comically disastrous results, sometimes with comically successful results. (Like pairing up a compulsive shopper with a kleptomaniac for an outing at the mall.) I don't agree with everything she says, but I will defend her right to say it – because she's hilarious!

"My favorite part was when she taught a high school girls' sex ed class that 70% of boys will lie to get sex, 80% won't use a condom, yet 90% are pro-life. She was reprimanded, of course. I think she should have gotten a medal.

"You will likely be offended at one point or another, but if you are secure enough to laugh at your own sacred cows instead of just everyone else's, this is a must read." weikelm, Librarything

"Wonderful read, funny, sarcastic. Loved it!" Charlie, Smashwords

"I just loved this book. It was a quick read, and left me in stitches. ..." Robin McCoy-Ramirez

"First, let me just say I was glad I was not drinking anything while reading this. I refrained from that. My husband said he never heard me laugh so much from reading a book. At one point, I was literally in tears. Jass Richards is brilliant with the snappy comebacks and the unending fountain of information she can spout forth. ... The quick wit, the sharp tongue, the acid words and sarcasm that literally oozes from her pores... beautiful." M. Snow, My Chaotic Ramblings

A Philosopher, a Psychologist, and an Extraterrestrial Walk into a Chocolate Bar

"Jass Richards is back with another great book that entertains and informs as she mixes feminism, critical thinking, and current social issues with humour ... The wedding intervention was hilarious. ..." James M. Fisher, *The Miramichi Reader*

"I found myself caught between wanting to sit and read [*A Philosopher, a Psychologist, and an Extraterrestrial Walk into a Chocolate Bar*] all in one go and wanting to spread it out. I haven't laughed that hard and gotten to spend time with such unflinchingly tough ideas at the same time. ... [And] the brilliance of the Alices! ... I can now pull out your book every time somebody tries to claim that novels can't have meaningful footnotes and references. [Thanks too] for pointing me to the brilliant essay series 'Dudes are Doomed.' I am eagerly watching for *The ReGender App* ..." C. Osborne

TurboJetslams: Proof #29 of the Non-Existence of God

"Extraordinarily well written with wit, wisdom, and laugh-out-loud ironic recognition, *TurboJetslams: Proof #29 of the Non-Existence of God* is a highly entertaining and a riveting read that will linger on in the mind and memory long after the little book itself has been finished and set back upon the shelf (or shoved into the hands of friends with an insistence that they drop everything else and read it!). Highly recommended for community library collections, it should be noted for personal reading lists." *Midwest Book Review*

"We all very much enjoyed it—it's funny and angry and heartfelt and told truly..." McSweeney's

"If you're looking for a reading snack that has zero saccharine but is loaded with just the right combination of snark, sarcasm, and humor, you've found it." Ricki Wilson, Amazon

"What Richards has done is brilliant. At first, I began getting irritated as I read about a familiar character, or a familiar scenario from our time living on the lake. Then, as the main character amps up her game, I see the thrill in the planning and the retribution she undertakes for pay back." mymuskoka.blogspot.ca/2016/07/book-review-turbojetslams.html

Substitute Teacher from Hell

"I enjoyed reading "Supply Teacher from Hell" immensely and found myself bursting out laughing many, many times. It is extremely well-written, clever, and very intelligent in its observations." Iris Turcott, dramaturge

more at jassrichards.com

Also by Jass Richards

fiction

(the Rev and Dylan series)
The ReGender App
License to Do That
The Blasphemy Tour
The Road Trip Dialogues

(the Brett series)
Dogs Just Wanna Have Fun
This Will Not Look Good on My Resume

A Philosopher, a Psychologist, and an Extraterrestrial Walk into a Chocolate Bar

TurboJetslams: Proof #29 of the Non-Existence of God

stageplays
Substitute Teacher from Hell

screenplays
Two Women, Road Trip, Extraterrestrial

performance pieces
Balls

nonfiction
Jane Smith's Translation Dictionary

Too Stupid to Visit

and other collections of funny bits

Jass Richards

Magenta

Too Stupid to Visit
and other collections of funny bits
© 2021 Jass Richards

www.jassrichards.com
jassrichards@gmail.com

978-1-926891-89-7 (paperback)
978-1-926891-90-3 (epub)
978-1-926891-91-0 (pdf)

Published by Magenta

Magenta

Cover photo #136468297 © Believeinme | Dreamstime.com
Print interior design and ebook formatting by Elizabeth Beeton

All rights reserved. Without limiting the rights under copyright reserved above, no part of this publication may be reproduced, stored in or introduced into a retrieval system, or transmitted, in any form, or by any means (electronic, mechanical, photocopying, recording, or otherwise) without the prior written permission of both the copyright owner and the above publisher of this book.

Library and Archives Canada Cataloguing in Publication
Title: Too stupid to visit : and other collections of funny bits / Jass Richards.
Names: Richards, Jass, 1957- author.
Identifiers: Canadiana (print) 20210122366 | Canadiana (ebook) 20210122641 |
  ISBN 9781926891897 (softcover) | ISBN 9781926891903 (EPUB) |
  ISBN 9781926891910 (PDF)
Subjects: CSH: Canadian wit and humor (English)
Classification: LCC PS8635.I268 T66 2021 | DDC C818/.602—dc23

Acknowledgements

Too Stupid to Visit

Thanks to …

William Sierichs, Jr., Woolsey Teller, and Marilyn Waring.

Born that Way

Thanks to …

Farrell Till ("What about Casualty Numbers" in *Skeptical Review* [Winter 1995: 8-9]) for bringing to my attention the information presented in the war stories bit.

Fern and Laurie Wayman for the intelligent design bit, the "How to find a wife" bit, and the godless heathens bit.

Julian Barnes for the other possibilities bit.

The Freedom from Religion Foundation ("Cookie Cutter Christs") for the Krishna, Mithra, Buddha, Quexalcote, and Indra bit.

Contents

Too Stupid to Visit 1

We Should Put a Crocodile in There 17

Born that Way 27

Let the Cows Loose 43

Jass Richards does Europe 49

Other Funny Bits 65

Too Stupid to Visit

Are there intelligent life forms out there in the universe?
Well yeah. No one's visited us yet.

•

If the history of the Earth were a year, life would not appear until March, multi-cellular organisms not until November. Dinosaurs would show up on December 13, and mammals on December 15. On December 31, we'd show up. By late evening, we'd have well-developed brains.

And then it'd take us 60 seconds to thoroughly trash the place.

•

We put tons of carcinogens into our food, water, and air.

And then spend millions of dollars looking for the cure for cancer.

Oh where oh where could it be.

•

The thing about cause and effect is that unless it's immediate and visual, we just don't get it. We just don't connect.

Consider CFCs and the ozone: it took us 10 years to figure that one out. It took us another 20 to do something about it, and it'll probably take *another* 20 to do something *effective*.

(Wear sunscreen. Good one.)

•

We sentenced Socrates to death and let a number of serial killers live.

•

We're still trying to get our whites whiter.

•

Jass Richards

We distinguish males from females. Before we do anything else. And before we do everything else. For example, '*Mr.* Smith' really means '*Penis-Person* Smith'. The use of such sex-identifying prefixes is considered polite. The use of 'Penis-Person' – or 'Dickhead' – is not.

Apparently.

•

Heard this guy say the other day that women can't do jobs that involve heavy machinery.

You don't have to *lift* it, you just have to *operate* it!

Besides – forklift.

•

Most men generally don't think much of most women.

And yet, they continue to prohibit them from joining the military, where they could easily get killed.

•

This is our defence policy: I'll hit you so you can't hit me so I can't hit you so you can't hit me ...

•

Our foreign aid policy goes something like this: the adults are too weak to do much of anything and the kids are so malnutritioned they're mentally retarded, but hey, let's give them just enough food (and no contraception) so they can keep on reproducing, a million new kids every three weeks.

•

A contraceptive pill designed for men was rejected because of the negative side-effect of reducing their sex drive.

Too Stupid to Visit

Given the reason for taking the pill, wouldn't that have been a positive side-effect?

•

We live in a world in which countries routinely sell weapons to their enemies: "Hey you. Yeah you. I'm gonna blow your face off. Yeah. What? You got nothin' to fight with? Hey Vinny, sell the man one of your bazookas. No, not that one, the other one. Yeah. Well he can pay us later. Put him on our don't-pay-till-May plan. Okay? You all set now? Okay then. *Now* I'm gonna blow your face off."

•

The Training Center for Subversive Warfare teaches that "Torture must be kept clean, it must not be carried out in the presence of those with sadistic tendencies, it must be carried out by some responsible person, and above all, it must be humane."

Otherwise, it would be, what, wrong?

•

McMaster University initiated a research project to study the health effects of war.

Perhaps some genius hypothesized that it causes death.

•

In a recent experiment involving monkeys, 13% pulled a chain electroshocking an unrelated monkey whose agony was in plain view. In a similar experiment conducted with humans, 65% administered the shock, to the point of fatality.

Much to do was subsequently made about the ethics – of the experimenters.

•

Jass Richards

Many of us are too unimaginative – or too lazy – or both – to make our lives worthwhile. So we have kids. That's our contribution to society. Genetic replications of our deficiency.

This inability to find fulfillment in the here and now is shared by those who set their sights on some heaven. No surprise, they're the ones with the most kids.

·

A worker, no doubt somebody's kid, accidentally dropped a socket wrench down a silo. It hit a missile causing an explosion that launched a nine megaton hydrogen bomb into a field several hundred yards away. Oops.

Because of naval mishaps, there are now nine nuclear reactors and fifty nuclear warheads on the ocean floor. Mishaps.

A nuclear bomb fell out of a U.S. bomber and landed in a Carolina swamp. It has not yet been found. Perhaps the localized proliferation of two-headed alligators should be considered a clue.

The U.S. dropped four plutonium bombs on Spain by mistake. I have to ask: four at once or on four separate occasions?

·

The Annual Turing Test Competition is an event in which a panel of experts asks questions from a remote location of a bunch of computers and a bunch of people. If they can't tell that a computer *is* a computer, it passes the Turing Test: it is deemed able to think.

In a recent competition, some of the people failed the test.

·

A sign on a community bulletin board saying "Learn to read English – Classes held Monday nights!" was posted by the Board of Education.

Too Stupid to Visit

•

Some of our best and brightest philosophers have spent years trying to convince us that time doesn't exist.

•

The U.S. continues to puzzle over the persistence of racism. It also continues to call the official residence of the President 'The White House'.

•

Lieutenant General Daniel Graham once said, "If a one megaton bomb was about to explode over this building and you had the good sense to start walking and get behind a lilac bush, that bomb would not hurt you."

He was later chosen to be the Senior Military Advisor to the President.

•

In our species, sexual desire seems to induce a state of temporary idiocy.

Which is why it is not particularly encouraging that the male half of the species actually brags about being in a constant state of sexual readiness.

•

In Saudi Arabia, a woman must be accompanied by a man whenever she appears in public; otherwise, she is subject to torture.

Otherwise?

•

North Americans spend five billion dollars each year on special diets.

When it would be far cheaper to just move to Africa.

It costs more than $115,000 to create a job in crude oil production. It costs only $20,000 to create a job in solar energy production. We have an unemployment problem. We have an energy problem.

And, apparently, a math problem.

•

One country, fearing the loss of cheap oil, which happened to be located in another country, dropped bombs on that country, seeming to forget for a moment that oil was, well, flammable.

Not to worry. The other country remembered: fearing the loss of control over their oil, they set fire to it.

•

We came up with the concept of 'garbage': stuff we don't want *here* – so we put it *there*. All gone!

•

One of our richest banks sponsors the World Cross-Country Championship and watches runners from Kenya and Ethiopia, two countries crippled by debt interest and therefore starving, compete against each other – for the $100,000 that's dangling at the finish line.

•

The economic system used for decision-making by the United Nations, the World Bank, the International Monetary Fund, and national governments considers only cash-generating activities to be productive. So Tendai, who lives in Zimbabwe and spends eighteen hours a day providing food, clothing, and shelter for herself and her children, is unproductive. But Bubba, who sits on a nuclear missile for eight hours a day waiting for an order to push a button and destroy the planet – he's productive.

Too Stupid to Visit

•

For most of us, loss is the difference between what you have at Time 1 and what you have at Time 2: yesterday, I had ten marbles; today, I have seven; so I lost a few. Three, to be exact.

However, those in business define loss as the difference between what you get and what you might've gotten. So if they get ten marbles and they think they could've gotten a hundred, they 'suffer a loss' of ninety marbles.

Which means, by their own reckoning, they've lost quite a few more marbles than the rest of us.

•

Being male is very much about being in control.

One has to wonder, therefore, why they hang their entire 'manhood' on some one thing over which they have no voluntary control whatsoever.

(And they say they're the logical ones.)

•

Pitch for a sci-fi movie: A plague kills all the women on Earth except five, who manage to escape infection. On these five depend the continuation of the human species.

And when the men find them, it takes all of fifteen minutes to rape them to death.

(A very short sci-fi movie.)

•

Gaybashing? "Queers are disgusting! Men touching other men, that's really sick!"

Jass Richards

So yeah, go beat 'em up. Get real close and touch 'em all over.

"And AIDS is their fault, they should be quarantined!"

Maybe you can split a lip or bloody a nose — exchange a few bodily fluids while you're at it.

•

When AIDS became an epidemic, a certain company recalled the condoms not up to their new standards, claiming 'a certain social responsibility'.

Apparently they were unaware that people had been using their condoms not only to prevent the transmission of disease, but also to prevent the transmission of sperm.

(Which, yes, okay, could be considered the same thing ...)

•

Women, as a matter of routine, redden their lips, ornament their ears, push up their breasts, display their legs, and arch their feet.

Then they get pissed off if you see them as sex objects.

And they get *really* pissed off if you then tell they're being irrational.

•

I think the science of mascara has gone as far as it needs to go. All those women in the tv ads are so — *happy* — that their *eyelashes* can now be ultra-*curled*, ultra-*lengthened*, and ultra-*thickened*.

I dunno. If *my* eyes were that vacant, I sure wouldn't want to draw attention to them.

No wait a minute. If I were *that vacant* — I guess I *would*.

•

Too Stupid to Visit

The word 'wife' first referred to those women who were captured, after the invasion and conquest of a neighbouring tribe, and brought home to be slaves. 'To have and to hold' is in fact a legal expression used to transfer possession of a piece of property. In Canada, one in four wives is severely beaten during the course of the marriage; half of all wife assault victims are kicked in the abdomen when pregnant; and almost sixty percent of the women who are murdered are murdered by their husband.

And yet, get this: ninety-four percent of all women *consent* to get married.

·

Many men express surprise and puzzlement upon hearing the words "I'm pregnant."

Apparently many of us still haven't connected having sex with having babies.

·

Know why men are built so sex takes under ten minutes?

So as not to exceed their attention span.

·

And who came up with the name Viagra?

I guess it's supposed to sound like Niagara.

But it's Niagara *Falls*.

Better to have chosen Geyser.

'Course that sounds too much like Geezer.

I think they should've avoided that line of imagery altogether and gone with something like *Hamburger Helper*.

·

The team of genetic researchers that successfully cloned a sheep from a single adult cell named the sheep 'Dolly', after a certain large-breasted country singer, because that cell had come from a mammary gland.

Grown men, brilliant men, men on the cutting edge of science, men who become headline news, are quite likely still forcing farts at the dinner table and snickering about it.

•

A lot of people are against cloning humans because it'll take away our individuality.

Our what?

•

I heard someone say the other day, "Wouldn't it be great if we could travel through time?"

Hello. We travel from yesterday to today – every day.

•

In the workplace, merit is seldom rewarded.

But that's probably just because it's seldom recognized.

•

Over half of our planet's scientists and engineers work for the military.

The other half work for Pizza Pizza.

•

Two bombs in a building were set to go off an hour apart, and the Mayor of the City said, "The second bomb was clearly designed to hurt the rescue workers coming to assist, so we're dealing with a warped mind here."

Too Stupid to Visit

Um, wouldn't the first bomb kind of establish that?

•

Half the world's population is under twenty-five. The ones who aren't undernourished are crack babies or fetal alcohol syndrome babies or AIDS babies or babies who for no good reason reached adolescence and graduated from high school but can't spell 'graduated'.

Makes you want to go right out and buy one of those 'Children are Our Future' posters.

•

We make toy guns, encouraging our kids to play at killing each other.

•

In the spring of 1991, Fred Turner set out from Beaufort, South Carolina, to walk across America in order to prove that most people are good.

He got as far as the state line before he was robbed and pushed off a bridge.

•

We have an irrational obsession with being first. The first to land on the moon. The first to discover insulin.

The first to find that landmine.

Most of the time, it's not true anyway. I mean, do we really think Roger Bannister was the first person to run a mile in under four minutes?

Talk to the guy who *wasn't* Cheetah's lunch.

•

We did heroic things to save three whales caught in the ice with insufficient oxygen.

Otherwise, they would never have gotten the chance to experience a long, slow death from PCB poisoning.

•

There have been over 1900 tests of nuclear weapons since World War II.

You'd think we'd get it right after, say, the first couple hundred.

And we haven't figured out yet what to do with the leftover stuff. We have enough radioactive waste to contaminate all of the Earth's lakes and rivers – twice. Canada alone has enough to stack a six-foot-high pile along the TransCanada Highway from coast to coast. We don't know what to do with the stuff. But we keep making it.

We tossed some of it into the ocean. But apparently it doesn't just dissolve.

We launched some of it into outer space. But now the insurance companies won't cover our space shuttles for collision.

We buried some of it in containers – that clearly won't last as long as the stuff itself.

And we used some of it to build schools and kitchen tables. Call it recycling.

Our favourite way to get rid of it, however, seems to be sneaking into some other country's back yard late at night, dumping it, and then running away.

•

I was reading the other day about this guy Daniel Maston, an assistant operator at the Point Lepreau Nuclear Generating Station, sentenced to four months for spiking the cafeteria's juice cooler with tritiated heavy water from the reactor.

Apparently he said – and I quote – "I don't have a good reason. I just did it. Maybe it was a joke."

Too Stupid to Visit

Who needs to worry about terrorists stealing plutonium with workers like that at our nuclear plants?

•

The site chosen for one particular nuclear power plant is two miles from an active fault line. *And* the blueprints for the reactors got mixed up, so the earthquake fault supports were installed backwards.

Oh yeah – we're definitely ready for that anti-matter stuff.

We Should Put a Crocodile in There

Most athletes are driven by the desire to win.

Not to win anything in particular, anything of significance, just – to win.

•

Olympic athletes are especially driven. Imagine spending *years* trying to throw a really heavy ball a few centimetres further than the next guy.

Now there's a candidate for the Lifetime Achievement Award.

•

I heard one athlete the other day emphasize the need to stay focussed and keep his objective in mind.

How hard can that be for a sprinter?

•

Speaking of which, one of the most lauded athletic feats is to run a hundred metres in under 10 seconds. The current record holder can do it in 9.58.

My *dog* can do better than that. And she's only six.

'Course, *she's* black too.

•

Have you noticed that more and more athletes are saying a quick prayer at the starting line?

A clear admission that you can't possibly win without divine intervention – yeah, that'll really psych out your opponents.

•

Another thing I've noticed is that the distance running events are always won by someone from Kenya, Ethiopia, or some other starving country.

See what you can do when all you've got to carry around is skin-and-bones?

·

Know why it took a while for there to be a women's triple jump?

Because hopscotch isn't really a challenge for us anymore.

Know what event I'd like to see?

Men's double-dutch.

·

Apparently from now on, athletes who test positive for marijuana, a performance-*diminishing* drug, are actually *prohibited* from competing in their sport.

Provided they can remember what it is.

·

On a similar note, a certain snowboarder will be disqualified as soon as he stops saying "Woh, dude!" and gets off the chairlift, and a certain archery competitor will be disqualified if he ever gets the arrow, string, and bow thing figured out.

·

You know how there are different weight classes in wrestling? I think other sports should do that too. For example, in the high jump, there should be a separate competitive class for short guys.

·

Too Stupid to Visit

It's interesting – okay, fucking *amusing* – to compare men's and women's sports. For example, in gymnastics, one of the women's events is the balance beam. They do these aerial cartwheel somersault things, on a four-inch wide beam, set three feet off the floor.

The *men's* big balance move is ... on the floor. It's a front scale. Basically, they stand on one foot. "Look at me, I can stand on one foot!"

It's hard to say which of the two is more ... thought-provoking.

And the men don't even do their floor stuff to music. I guess that would be too difficult, too distracting.

Or maybe the gymnastics federation is afraid that adding music to the men's floor would attract athletes who ... can dance.

And the high bar. One bar. Ooooh. Try flipping around *two* of them. Set at different heights.

Incidentally, know why women gymnasts are so young?

Because nobody with a fully developed *mind* would even *try* half the stuff they do. (You want me to do what? Umm ... no. Don't think so.)

And volleyball. When the women dive for the ball, they do this really neat shoulder roll: it's smooth, quick, and cool to see.

The men's technique? They do a bellyflop onto the floor. Really, it's sort of a chest-first body slam. They probably think it looks heroic.

I think it looks – stupid.

•

Did you know we once tried a men's synchronized swimming team? But one guy got pissed off at another guy, and then another guy got involved, and next thing you know, half the team's dead in the water.

Guess they just couldn't handle that hold-hands-and-coordinate thing.

Jass Richards

•

Every now and then – usually when women approach or surpass men's performance – men will proclaim "Sports are too dangerous for women! They might get hurt!"

This from the sex that routinely gets black eyes, split lips, sprained muscles, torn ligaments, dislocated joints, broken bones, and nerve damage. From sports.

The sex that has its reproductive vitals hanging by a thread at the body's bull's-eye with nary a centimetre of fat for protection. And voluntarily competes on the aptly named pommel horse.

Need I point out that women's musculature is generally more elastic, rendering it less prone to injury?

And that women seem to have a better developed survival instinct? We duck. We run the fuck the other way. And we don't make insupportable claims about the sexual preferences of our opponents' parents.

•

How many swimmers does it take to change a light bulb?

Don't know yet. They keep getting electrocuted.

•

Why did the cyclist cross the road?

To get to the finish line.

•

I've noticed that in men's figure skating, the warrior theme is very common. Even artsy skaters like the American Todd Eldredge have done it.

Too Stupid to Visit

Is it wise to act out killing someone, with pride, and celebration, at a meet where all of your fellow competitors, including those from oh, I don't know – Russia, Japan, Israel – have easy access to a pair of sharp blades?

Figure skating commentators completely miscall the pairs event, by the way.

He doesn't *lift* her; she *balances*.

He doesn't *throw* her; she *soars*.

And what's noteworthy is not that he catches her, but that she doesn't slice off anything in the process.

•

Basketball. Now *there's* a great sport. The Harlem Globetrotters are living proof that the human hand was *made* to handle a ball.

Which is why *soccer* is such a stupid sport.

Then again, basketball *used to be* a great sport. Have you seen that new NBA player? The one that can dunk the ball just by reaching over from centre court?

•

There are a few sports we just haven't named very well.

Squash is not played with a squash.

There are no fences in fencing and no rugs in rugby.

And the butterfly – have you ever *seen* what happens to a butterfly in water?

•

And there are a few I don't understand. In weight lifting, people lift heavy stuff. They don't take it anywhere. They don't do anything with it. They just pick it up and then put it back down.

Badminton involves swatting, back and forth through the air with speed and strategic aim, an object that has been designed with total disregard for the principles of aerodynamics as they pertain to speed and directional control.

The shooting part of the biathlon involves targets that stand still.

Strategy in football amounts to "Fake left, go right."

'Course when your opponents have such short attention spans, that's probably sufficient.

On a regular basis, men will enter a ring and punch each other repeatedly in the head. This causes brain damage.

Well, *more* brain damage.

Critics are reminded that the participants are consenting adults.

That's the part I don't get.

•

And there are several sports in which we haven't yet reached our full potential.

For example, in bowling – okay, let's just say for now it's a sport – in bowling, you should get extra points for knocking down pins in the other lanes.

After skiers race down the hill, they should have to turn around and race back up.

In water polo, as in regular polo, there should be horses involved.

Too Stupid to Visit

In the sculls, they should narrow the lanes and let the competitors whack their opponents out of their boats.

The flimsy crossbar of the pole vault should be replaced with a sturdy two-by-four. That's nailed in place.

In the 400m relay, instead of a baton, they should have to pass off a chicken.

And in the steeplechase, in that pool of water after that last hurdle? We should put a crocodile in there.

Born that Way

Most of us still think there's a god.

Well, okay, maybe that's not really a problem.

We still think it's an all-wise and all-good god.

·

We pray to this god.

But he's omniscient – he already knows what we're going to say.

And it's not like we're going to change his mind: Hey, Supreme Being and Ruler of the Universe – this is what *I* think should happen here.

·

Besides which, there's something fundamentally wrong with prayer.

It doesn't work.

·

Most people figure either God exists or he doesn't. But there are other possibilities.

Maybe he used to exist, but he doesn't anymore. Maybe he got run over by a truck or something.

Or maybe he does exist, but he's abandoned us. We may have been a disappointment. Or an infectious disease. Maybe he inherited us. Or got us for Christmas. And he's still trying to give us back. Or exchange us.

Or maybe he exists, but he went on holiday and got lost because, like one of his favourite sons who took the forty-year desert tour, he doesn't know how to stop and ask for directions.

·

A neuropsychologist, Michael A. Persinger, has discovered that when certain parts of the brain are stimulated with a small electrical current, 'god experiences' occur: people report feeling a divine presence and hearing God's voice. Surely that's proof that so-called religious experiences are just biochemical burps.

Either that or God's just messin' with us.

•

Ever wonder why he doesn't just once and for all provide conclusive evidence that he exists? Something simple and yet – godly.

Nothing weird like throwing chunks of bread at us.

•

Pascal figured that if there is a god and a heaven, and you *don't* believe, you don't get in; but if there isn't a god or a heaven, and you *do* believe, well, nothing of it. So it's a safer bet to believe that God exists.

Okay, but what if there *is* a god and heaven's only for those smart enough to recognize there's no proof that he exists?

•

In any case, I don't think they should give drivers' licenses to people who believe in life after death.

•

Krishna, an ancient god, was born of a virgin twelve hundred years before Jesus Christ. He was visited by wise men at his birth, he performed miracles, and he was crucified.

Mithra, another ancient god, was also born of a virgin, on December 25, six hundred years before Christ. He was visited by wise men at his birth, and his first followers were shepherds (he had twelve in particular). He was crucified, and then he ascended into heaven.

Buddha too was born of a virgin, six hundred years before Christ. He too performed miracles and was crucified; he descended into Hades for three days, and then he ascended into heaven.

Quexalcote, another god, was also born of a virgin, five hundred and eighty-seven years before Christ. He spent forty days fasting and resisting temptation, was crucified, along with two thieves, and was resurrected three days later.

Indra, yet another god, was born of a virgin, walked on water, was crucified, and then ascended into heaven.

Now, is all that just coincidence or what?

·

And about this so-called 'intelligent design': tornadoes don't have guidance systems, we don't have earlids, and pain hurts more than it needs to.

·

But, well, God works in mysterious ways.

Why is that again?

·

The state motto of Ohio is "With God, all things are possible."

Oh yeah? Is it possible for him to create a rock so heavy he can't lift it?

·

The Bible continues to appear on bestseller lists even though the plot is confusing, the characters are unlikeable, the dialogue, unrealistic, and the tone, juvenile.

And much of it is just fucking incoherent. "Wherefore my sentence is, that we trouble not them, which from among the Gentiles are turned to God" (Acts 15:19). What the hell does that even *mean*?

•

Many people blame Eve for disobeying God and eating the apple. But how could she have known that was wrong? The apple was from the tree of the *knowledge* of good and evil – so until she ate it, she didn't *know* right from wrong!

And anyway, why did God forbid knowledge of good and evil? Could it be he didn't want us to know what an evil messed up sonuvabitch he was? Given that he proceeded to order mass murders left, right, and center – the Hittites, the Girgashites, the Amorites, the Canaanites, the Perizzites, the Hivites, the Jebusites, and the entire cities of Makkadah, Libnah, Lachish, Gezer, Eglon, and Hebron – and we *still* think he's overflowing with love and kindness, well, he obviously didn't have anything to worry about.

In any case, because of this knowledge of good and evil thing, we're born sinners.

So what, blessed are the psychopaths?

•

And this notion of being born in a state of 'original sin' – just by being born, you're bringing sin into the world.

Sort of puts abortion in a *good* light, doesn't it?

•

Who was Cain's wife? I mean, if it was Eve, then we're the result of inbreeding all the way back – which, now that I think of it, explains a lot.

And if it was someone else – *who* created *her*?

Too Stupid to Visit

•

The Great Flood? Noah and all that? According to *The Bible*, the water rose 15 cubits and covered the mountains (Gen 7:20).

One cubit is about a foot and a half, so 15 cubits would be about 25 feet.

Those are some awfully high mountains.

(And *our* god created those?)

•

I've been reading some of the war stories in *The Bible* and apparently some guy named Adino killed 800 men in a single battle, and Abishai and Jashobeam each killed 300 (2 Sam 23:8,18; 1 Chr 11:11). Who were these guys? I mean, even if that single battle lasted a full 24 hours, that's at least 12 killed per hour – which is one guy every five minutes. Now I've never killed a person, with just knives and swords and shit, but it can't be that easy. One guy every five minutes for 24 hours straight?

In another battle, the Israelites killed 120,000 people in one day. During World War II, the Germans, along with the allied forces, using heavy tanks, artillery, mortars, machine guns, hand grenades, landmines, fighter planes, and bombs, managed to kill only 176,000 people over a period of six weeks.

So inquiring minds have to ask: when these guys went fishing, did they ever catch anything? Yeah? How big was it?

•

In addition to the forementioned, according to Biblical accounts, God commanded the deaths of 185,000 Assyrians, 120,000 Midianites, 120,000 Judeans, 100,000 Syrians, 24,000 Israelites, and 10,000 Moabites.

He's obviously rounding off to the nearest thousand, and I have to tell you, that lack of attention to detail bothers me.

·

Here's The Biblical Guide to Finding that Special Someone:

Find an attractive prisoner of war, take her home, shave her head, trim her nails, and give her new clothes. Then she's yours. (Deut 21:11-13)

When you see someone you like, go home and tell your parents to get her for you. (Judg 14:2).

Go to a party and hide. When the women come out to dance, grab one and carry her off to be your wife. (Judg 21; 19-25)

Find a man with several daughters and impress him by watering his flock. Or cutting off the foreskins of two hundred of his enemies. (Ex 2:16-21; 1 Sam 18:27)

·

Their infants shall be dashed in pieces and their women with child shall be ripped up (Hos 13:16).

Happy shall he be, that taketh and dasheth thy little ones against the stones (Ps 137:9).

They shall have no pity on the fruit of the womb (Isa 13:18).

Dash their children and rip up their women with child (2 Kgs 8:12).

Thou shalt eat the fruit of thine own body (Deut 28:53).

So I guess he's not really Pro-Life then, is he.

·

And O Creator of Everything, how can you not once even *mention* DNA? (Not in Genesis, not in Revelation ...)

·

Too Stupid to Visit

I used to be pissed because none of the disciples were women. Then I realized what a sorry lot of gullible schmucks they were, traipsing along after a total stranger, leaving at a moment's notice their families and their jobs – "Hey, come follow me! I'm God! No, really! Look – there, I've made a bush burn!"

·

Thou shalt not kill. (Ex 20:13) Put every man his sword by his side and slay his brother, companion, and neighbour. (Ex 32:27)

Thou shalt not make any likeness of anything that is in heaven. (Ex 20:4) Thou shalt make two cherubims of gold. (Ex 25:18)

For by grace are ye saved through faith, not by works. (Eph 2:8,9) By works a man is justified, and not by faith. (Jas 2:24)

I am a jealous God visiting the iniquity of the fathers upon the children unto the third and fourth generations. (Ex 20:5) The son shall not bear the iniquity of the father. (Ezek 18:20)

Peace I leave with you, my peace I give unto you. (Jn 14:27) Think not that I am come to send peace on earth. (Mt 10:34)

Submit yourself to every ordinance of man. (1 Pet 2:13) We ought to obey God rather than men. (Acts 5:29)

Looks like they're right – he *does* transcend the rules of logic.

·

Or maybe he just changes his mind a lot.

Every moving thing that liveth shall be meat for you (Gen 9:3); no, wait, ye shall not eat of them that chew the cud or of them that divide the cloven hoof (Deut 14:7).

I am merciful, and I will not keep anger forever (Jer 3:12). Ye have kindled a fire in mine anger, which shall burn forever (Jer 17:4). Well, which is it?

Or could be he's just wrong a lot.

He said that Adam would die on the day he ate the apple (Gen 2:16,17), but he didn't (Gen 3:17; Gen 5:3).

He told Jehoiakim that he wouldn't have a son (Jer 36:30), but he did (2 Kgs 24:6).

·

Or maybe he just lies a lot.

He promised Jacob that he would return from Egypt (Gen 46:3,4), but he didn't – he died there (Gen 49).

They shall seek me early, but they shall not find me (Prov 1:28); nope, I lied – these that seek me early *shall* find me (Prov 8:17).

Whatever, "God said so!" doesn't mean dick-all, does it?

·

Chapter 28 of Deuteronomy says that if we don't hearken unto God's voice, he's going to smite us with consumption, fever, inflammation, burning, hemorrhoids, the scab, the itch, and the botch of Egypt.

The botch of Egypt?

·

And God created us in his image.

·

Speaking of creation, if God made everything, who made God?

If he just *always was*, then why couldn't it be that everything else just *always was*?

Too Stupid to Visit

And if he *made* him*self*, well, I guess that means he *can* go fuck himself!

•

Speaking of which, the Pope says that if a man with HIV can't abstain from intercourse, it's better that he infect his wife than use a condom.

And I say that if a woman with PMS can't resist a rage, it's better that she gun down the Pope than take a Midol.

•

Anti-gun law advocate and pastor of the New Life Christian Fellowship, Herbert Kershaw, accidentally shot himself to death while demonstrating gun safety to his family.

I think it's time for some new reps.

President Bush keeps talking about his "personal relationship with Jesus".

Which is odd, because the last time I talked to Jesus – yesterday – he said he didn't know him.

•

Ever notice how similar religion and sex are?

They both promise transcendence, ecstasy. (They both fail to deliver, but that's another point.)

They both involve salvation: one looks to God like one does to a lover, for redemption. (Again, they both – never mind.)

They both involve a little sadomasochism, a little bondage and discipline: more than one saint has submitted to flagellation, and isn't every monk given a hairshirt and every nun her own little whip?

And of course, to kneel in prostration is to put one's ass in the air – I'm ready, enter me, Oh Great One.

•

Speaking of which, it seems to me God's a little obsessed with sex – there are so many stories in *The Bible* of rape, incest, whoring, lust, coveting thy neighbour's wife, deflowering virgins ...

He's also a little obsessed with food – what to eat, when to eat ...

I guess that's what happens when you're non-corporeal.

•

I read the other day that Vision TV, a religious network, won't accept ads for alcoholic beverages or feminine hygiene products.

Well that makes sense: I mean, we all know what a good buzz you can get from a tampon.

•

People give $80 million a day to God. $80 million a day!

Just what the fuck has he been doing with all that money?

And when do you think he'll start paying taxes for roads, schools, hospitals, and stuff?

•

Those people who become 'born again' – I guess that's *one* way to avoid growing up.

•

Why did the guardian angel cross the road?

To be with his imaginary friend.

Too Stupid to Visit

•

Studies have shown that people who go to church are happier than those who do not.

Okay, and people who take Prozac are happier still.

•

Speaking of which, apparently a bunch of people looked up at the sky one day and saw the clouds shaped into a happy face. They said it was a sign from God.

What it was a sign *of*, they didn't say.

•

Studies have also shown that religion doesn't much determine whether or not people will be good Samaritans.

The weather does.

•

I was talking to some non-practising Catholics the other day.

Told them I was a non-practising saint.

•

A church group at the University of Texas is promoting Christian faith as the best way to avoid abduction by aliens.

Well yeah. Any aliens that come here won't be *that* stupid.

(Then again, any aliens that come *here* –)

•

I was in the store the other day and I sneezed, and someone called out cheerfully, "Bless you!"

Good thing. I'd hate to lose my soul out my nose. I'm glad God's available to see to that.

•

Another someone came to my door one day and asked whether I'd found Jesus.

I said, "No, and I have to say I'm not impressed with a saviour who plays hide-and-seek."

•

Have you seen those lawn signs? "A Christian Family lives here. We have kept the Christ in Christmas."

And missed the sermon on pride.

•

And did you hear about that Amish kid who got caught reading porn?

He parents confiscated his entire collection of *Car & Driver* and *Popular Mechanics*.

•

Isn't it interesting that the people who talk the loudest about family values are the ones who worship a dead-beat dad? I mean look, he left a couple thousand years ago. Said he'd be back real soon. Yeah right. "Wait 'till your father gets home." *That* got tired real quick. He never writes. He never calls. Child support? "Cheque's in the mail." Sure. Tell that to Africa.

•

You know how when there's a train wreck or something, survivors often attribute their good fortune to God – they walk around saying "It's a miracle! Praise the Lord!"

Too Stupid to Visit

That happened to me once. I was driving back from a business meeting with my pompous little shit of a supervisor and we got into a three-car pile-up. He was killed instantly and I said the same thing – "It's a miracle! Praise the Lord!"

·

Speaking of miracles, God can walk on water? We can race across it at a hundred miles an hour.

He can rise up to the clouds? Hell, we've been to the moon and back.

He can heal the sick? We can make them sick in the first place and *then* heal them.

He fed 5,000 people with just five loaves of bread? What, no fries with that?

He transformed water into wine? Check out what we've done with the Great Lakes.

The virgin birth? Duh. We *invented* the turkey baster.

He can resurrect the dead? Well that's just gross.

·

Investigators of yet another stigmata 'miracle' – blood seeping from the wounds of a crucified Christ figure – discovered that the red stuff was indeed genuine human blood.

Wouldn't that cast *doubt* on the 'son of a *god*' thing?

·

You know, we keep hearing that atheists are godless heathens gonna burn in hell. But it wasn't atheists who subjected a good number of people to assorted tortures during the Inquisition. It wasn't atheists who burned at the stake women suspected of flying through the air and having sex with Satan (not necessarily in that order). It wasn't atheists who herded Jews and Gypsies into boxcars during the German holocaust. It wasn't atheists in white sheets leading the lynch mobs. It wasn't atheists bombing abortion clinics and gay nightclubs. And it's not atheists hijacking planes and flying them into tall buildings full of people.

Singing "Here Comes Santa Claus" during the Lord's Prayer at City Council? Okay, yeah, that was us.

·

By the way, I don't understand all the anger about discontinuing 'The Prayer' in schools, courtrooms, council meetings, and other public places. We're not trying to stop you from praying wherever and whenever you want – we'd just rather you not be such an exhibitionist about it.

·

Did you hear about that guy who sued God? Maybe he lives in California and he suffered one too many 'Acts of God', I don't know, but I thought he had a pretty good case.

What would be God's defence? "I didn't know"? There goes omniscience. "I couldn't do anything"? There goes omnipotence. "I really just didn't give a fuck"? There goes beneficence.

My guess is he won't show. There goes existence.

·

And yet ... a recent poll found that almost 80% of North Americans are Christian.

They say they were born that way.

Let the Cows Loose

One day at the gas station, I saw a couple guys on their way to their hunt camp.

"How many squares did ya bring?" the one asked the other.

A case of 24 bottles of beer is not square. It's rectangular.

And God help us, they're the ones with all the spatial ability.

•

I don't understand hunting. I don't understand the desire to kill.

"Oh but it's not that," they say. "We like the meat."

Then why don't you just go out and shoot the nearest cow?

•

Speaking of which, have you heard that hunters are protesting elk farms? Because they're *unethical.*

Right. They're just pissed because the farmers are taking away their fun.

Well, fair's fair. I say let the cows loose.

•

And "It's gotta be wild!" they say.

Okay, how about a skunk?

"No, it's the excitement of stalking an animal that's big and wild, and can tear you apart."

Yeah right. Like Bambi's cousin's gonna tear you apart.

•

"And the challenge! Deer are smart, y'know!"

I guess it depends on who you're comparing them to.

I'd say the average deer has an IQ of what, three?

Besides, they hunt in a group, so already it's what, six against one? And they use dogs, hell, they even use helicopters to scare the animals out of the bush. And then they've got some geezer sitting in a truck parked at the side of the road just waiting to pick off the first one that runs across.

Then again, since said geezer's probably been chugging beer all afternoon, that *would* be a challenge.

•

One deer season, I saw some guy standing a few metres off the road in the bush, waiting, rifle ready. He'd obviously gotten a call on his cellphone from his buddy, deep in the bush on his ATV, or in his helicopter, flushing out the animals with dogs, hand grenades, and what have you.

"You're not gonna kill the mom and two little fawns we see around here, are you?" I asked.

"Oh, we'll try not to!" he smiled.

What's to try? Unload the gun.

If that's too tricky, just put it down.

Dumbfucks.

•

And I don't understand the wardrobe. You have the matching pants and shirt in camouflage 'I'm hiding' greens and browns, and the vest, gloves, and hat in the brightest 'I can't help but be seen' orange. The ensemble fairly *shouts* 'I'm a man.'

Too Stupid to Visit

•

Speaking of which, I was talking to one guy – a duck hunter – and I asked why he preferred to go hunting with a friend. He said, 'For security.'

I'm ascared of the ducks, Jimbob, make 'em stop quacking!

But it's a good thing for men to admit their fears. Ducks can be dangerous. I mean last year alone, how many hunters were killed by ducks?

•

I don't know why they just don't forget the bullets and use paint pellets instead. Like those soldier-of-fortune-wannabe games that lawyers play on the weekends.

I can just see it now: it's the end of the first day and all the animals are showing up at their favourite spot for a brewski all spattered with red, and blue, and yellow – just looking at each other, saying 'What the fuck?'

•

I was looking through a hardware store flyer one hunting season – you know, it's quite a business, hunting.

First, you've got your Super Premium 200 Proof Doe-in-Heat-Scent. This stuff is real special, it's "collected at the peak of the doe's hottest second estrous cycle".

How do they know it's her peak?

And who does the collecting?

And you've got your Deluxe Shoulder-Length Dressing Gloves. I'm thinking something in black satin, but no, these are "heavy duty poly gloves that help protect against mess, stains, and infectious diseases while dressing game". The picture shows a guy with his arm up a deer's ass – I guess he's "dressing game".

Is that kind of like "making love"?

And then you've got your Rusty Duck Lubricant.

Don't leave home without it.

Lastly, you've got your duck calls, your deer calls, and your moose calls – the CM3 Moose Call was apparently very good, but I understand there were a lot of hunting injuries that year.

Well what do you think's gonna happen when some moron stands in the middle of a forest during mating season and yells out in moose language 'Come fuck me now!'

·

Speaking of mounting, have you ever wondered why guys who fish mount the whole fish but guys who hunt mount only the head? I mean, if it's size that counts, well then let's hang the whole fucking moose on the wall.

·

And this 'bigger is better' thing – completely illogical.

Anyone can shoot a moose that's just standing there.

If you really wanna brag, hang a pair of chipmunk ears on your wall.

Jass Richards does Europe

People in business class and first class need to feel *important* and *special.*

So they get to board *ahead* of the rest of us.

Along with the other infants and small children.

•

The men in Sweden don't wear ties.

I don't know about you, but any country in which the men *don't* walk around wearing little nooses gets my vote.

Then again, given that most countries come nowhere near Sweden's 43% with regard to women in government – hell, they've had a woman president for years – well, the noose thing does provide a certain ... convenience.

•

Y'know, when you're travelling in different countries and people don't necessarily speak the language you do, you quickly realize it doesn't really matter whether you say "Thank you" or "Danke schoen" or "Merci" or "Tousen takk" – as long as you say something and smile, your gratitude will be appreciated and the other person will smile back.

So when I got off the bus at the stop for the train station kindly indicated by the driver to whom I'd shown my Eurail pass and then gestured helplessly out at the streets, I smiled at him and said, "Your children have fleas."

And sure enough, he smiled back, nodding happily.

•

But I didn't realize how difficult it'd be to do simple things like buy groceries when you don't know the language. I mean you don't need to know Italian or Greek, for example, to recognize a loaf of bread when you see one.

Well, I can tell you now that whipping cream goes much better in tea than buttermilk.

•

In Europe, every train station has pigeons – not just out on the platforms, but actually inside the station building. I saw this one pigeon actually ride the escalator: it flew up off the floor to avoid being stepped on and landed on the escalator handrail and then ... just ... took the ride up.

Another figured out that if it hung around the station entertainers – and I use that word loosely – it could get *a lot* of crumbs: people would stand and nibble as they listened to the guy with the accordion or whatever.

I saw it two days later and it had its own act doing aerial manoeuvres. I don't know where it got the hat from or the sign saying "Cruddy chunks of food much appreciated" but it beat the hell out of the accordion guy.

•

Even before I got to France and Italy – in fact, as soon as I got to Sweden and saw huge outdoor flower pots at the airport terminal and then sculptures and art videos in the subway stations – well, by comparison, one comes to realize just how much the aesthetic simply does not count here. It has no value whatsoever.

'Course you can't really blame us. DaVinci and Michelangelo – *those* guys didn't bring their talent, their vision, to the New World. No, we got the guy with the accordion. The one who thought it would be more lucrative to play on a ship than on a train. A ship full of people who've just spent their last penny on passage.

Too Stupid to Visit

•

Europe just doesn't have the junk food we do. I had a heck of a time finding Doritos.

Especially in, of all places, Amsterdam.

•

It's true that when you travel, your horizons get broadened. One time, there was a person sitting across from me on a train who was reading the proceedings from some conference. I thought history maybe, or sociology. Turns out it was the *Proceedings of the Fifth Annual International Congress on Boar Semen Preservation*. They have congresses on boar semen preservation? See, I didn't know that before.

•

When I walked along the famous Champs-Élysées, there was so much traffic whizzing by, must've been four lanes in each direction. Though the trees lining each side are cool. An especially nice view from the middle of the street. Which is where you get to stand if you don't race across doing your Marian Jones imitation when the light changes and the little green man in the crosswalk sign lights up.

Copenhagen, on the other hand, is *made* for pedestrians. It has lots of pedestrian-only spaces, the streets have these *really wide* sidewalks, and in Copenhagen, pedestrians *always* have the right of way. You can be crossing the street *anywhere* and the cars will stop for you.

They'll do that in Amsterdam too. Though that could be because you're apt to be crossing the street backwards. And giggling.

But in Paris, *cars* always have the right of way. Even if the little green man says it's okay to cross. Actually, in Paris the little green man says "Okay … you can try it if you like."

There was this one small group of tourists stranded on a concrete island divider at a corner – I don't know how they got there, but they couldn't get off – they couldn't cross the street in any direction because cars kept coming, really fast, and none of them slowed down, they didn't even seem to notice that there were people standing there, trying to cross.

Well, except for the guy who looked over and started laughing. I think maybe he might've noticed …

Eventually they had to send out some street-crossing officer to get us.

But by then we were so dehydrated, and a little disoriented or confused, a few of us refused to leave our little island. It had become safe, you see …

•

One of the shops on the Champs-Élysées is the travel agency for *Iran Air – The Airline of the Islamic Republic of Iran.*

I'll bet they're not doing much business these days.

Given the tendency of Islamic pilots to fly *into* buildings.

•

I noticed there were no garbage cans along the Champs-Élysées. Anywhere. And I thought, 'Well, *that's* wishful thinking.' I mean it's non-stop tourists.

A block later I realized they'd just said, 'The hell with it,' given a woman a go-cart, put a vacuum cleaner on it, and made it a full-time job.

•

I got so tired of getting lost though. It was bad enough that I kept getting lost on my way from my bed-and-breakfast to the museum or

Too Stupid to Visit

wherever it was I wanted to go to, but I started getting lost *in* the museums.

It's true. You *can* spend days in the Louvre …

I saw this one painting of a shipwreck, the central figure was on the beach dramatically draped over crates and sails and stuff in a pose of utter exhaustion – and I thought, 'Oh get a grip!'

As a species, we are so in love with ourselves – almost every single one of the sculptures and paintings I saw features *human* subjects. I saw a few horses, a rabbit or two, and an antelope, but they were usually dead. Or dying a very horrible death.

'Course it could just be that animals won't sit still long enough.

That could also explain why they're usually dead.

•

I also went to the Versailles Castle. The fireplace in one room was all set and ready to go with three *logs* – seven feet long, ten inches thick.

That'd take a lot of lighter fluid.

And the huge wall-to-wall murals of battle scenes – the 17th century version of *Terminator* on Imax, I guess.

And the beds – canopies, embroidery, feathers, gold, and a four-foot-high platform. Talk about pressure to perform.

The description says the castle is actually King Louis' hunting lodge "enlarged" by his son. I'll say.

I did wonder if they had chandelier insurance. If one of *those* things should happen to fall – Well, there'd be 98 chandeliers left …

•

Another thing I got tired of was deferring to people taking pictures. What *is* this obsession with taking pictures of everything? If you want *pictures* of these places, why not just buy the postcards in the ever-present souvenir shop? I swear some people took pictures of the postcards.

'Course why not – the postcards *always* look better than the real thing.

•

Remember Jules Verne? The guy who went around the world in 80 days?

He didn't have to deal with airports and train stations and ferries.

•

I saw a street musician (still in Paris), just clapping – in time, I guess – but I have no idea to what.

•

Travelling would be so much easier if we could just beam ourselves from point A to point B. You could be sitting in your living room and think, "Gee, I'd like to go to New York" – and then just beam yourself there.

'Course, we'd need traffic conductors. Otherwise, we'd be colliding into each other's beams and who knows who you'd be when you got there.

I mean, what if *your* beam crossed the beam of a Pekinese on its way to Chicago? You'd arrive in New York half-Pekinese.

•

So, four days and three nights after Paris, I was on Syros, one of the Greek islands.

I discovered when I rented a moped to get from my little fishing village into town – and back again at night – when it was dark – driving on the only road – a narrow winding road that went all the way up a mountain and then all the way down – that not only do the

Too Stupid to Visit

Greeks not have streetlights, they don't really have guard rails to keep you from going over the edge and plummeting to a certain death.

At the really scary sections, they might have a few posts. No cable connecting the posts, just the posts. About, oh, how wide is a moped? That far apart.

And one section did have a low stone wall that I thought could act like a barrier. Apparently three other people thought the same thing. But they were wrong. And left three crumbling gaps as proof.

•

Some officials can be *so* unhelpful. While I was in town, I stopped at the ferry office to find out when ferries went from Syros to Santorini. There was a schedule posted outside, but that route wasn't listed. So I went inside and asked the ferry office person whether, and when, a ferry went from Syros to Santorini. She directed me to the posted schedule.

So I went back outside and read it again, and again, looking carefully at each of thirty different trips for three different ferries on seven different days leaving at six different times. Nothing from Syros to Santorini. I went back inside.

"Is that the schedule for *all* ferries?" I asked. Yes.

"Does the schedule change from week to week?" No.

"Does the schedule list all islands stopped on the way?" Yes.

Finally, the question I eventually asked – which wasn't among my first twenty – was "Is there another name for Santorini?" Sure enough, there it was: Syros to Thera, Mondays, Wednesdays, and Fridays, at 7:00 a.m.

•

So Friday, I headed down to a beach. A beach on Santorini. And just where I wanted to lay down my towel – midway between the screaming kids on the left and the bickering couple on the right – there were four small rocks. Just four. So I picked them up and tossed them away (two to the left and two to the right).

I lay down my towel and immediately the wind whipped it up. I'd get two corners down and half the towel smoothed out, and then as soon as I got the other two corners down, the first two would get blown up. Eventually I thought, 'Hey! I need something to hold down the corners! I know! Rocks! Four small ones!'

•

Why is it that people who in their normal lives wouldn't venture to walk around the block decide when on holiday to sign up for an excursion climb up a volcano. And show up wearing flipflops, sandals, and heels. Normally, I wouldn't object. Everyone has the right to be an idiot.

But not when it means the thirty-eight people behind you on the single-file path have to stop in the hot sun while you negotiate a ten inch step up from one rock to another.

I mean, it's not like you were caught by surprise and thus ill-prepared: if you sign up for "an excursion climb up a volcano" you should've known it would involve … climbing up a volcano.

And then there's the guy who has the right footwear – heavy duty basketball shoes – but he's so cool he hasn't done up the laces.

Watch how cool I am when he turns his ankle and asks for help to get back down.

And there's the guy who's mistaken the excursion for a race and attempts to pass everyone. At great risk not only to himself, which

Too Stupid to Visit

doesn't bother me, but to everyone he passes. When he finds himself behind a small group of women, well, you'd think he's never been so *insulted* – to see the look on his face and the determination with which he passes them.

I almost bump him off. But the volcano wasn't active at the time.

•

I have to say that the train ride from Athens to Patras was *really* annoying. For five hours. Not only because of the steady drone and rattle – that's *two different* annoying sounds by the way – but also because of the almost continuous blowing of the horn. Up to seven times a minute. I swear the conductor blew it even when we were nowhere near an intersection with a road. I figure he must've been one of those kids who wanted to be a train conductor when he grew up.

Eventually, recalling my moped night ride from hell, I realized it's the Greek custom to honk every time you approach a curve – which makes sense when everyone drives in the middle of the road – which they do because the roads aren't wide enough for you to drive on one side – unless you're driving a donkey. That said, I'm not sure what the train conductor thought might be coming at us from around each curve that needed warning. And frankly I was afraid to ask.

•

Once I got to Patras, I took a ferry to another island, Kefalonia. And while there, I decided to go for a walk to see a cave with stalactites and stalagmites. It was September, so the temperature was about 40 degrees. Centigrade. That's about 100 Fahrenheit. What can I say, I felt like going for a walk.

Actually, I felt like going for a run, but I'm not stupid.

So I started out on this 5 km walk – about 3 miles – at about the time all good Greeks start their mid-afternoon siesta: the heat stroke time of day.

That Greek guy who ran the first marathon and then dropped dead? I always figured he died of a heart attack or something. Uh-uh.

He died of embarrassment, what with all the locals laughing at him for even *attempting* such a thing.

Did I wear sunscreen? Not me, I tan, I don't burn.

Did I take water? Nope. I regularly run 10 miles without a water stop.

I *did* wear white. Which is a good thing. Because it makes you more noticeable to passing motorists when you've collapsed at the side of the road.

•

As a philosophy student, I'd always wanted to see olive groves, perhaps walk among them deep in thought. Well, I thought, as I walked along the road on this Greek island, I have now seen olive trees. At least, trees with what are almost certainly olives-to-be, olives-in-progress, *potential* olives.

Whether I've seen olive *groves*, however, depends on how many trees constitute a grove.

I bet *that's* a question Plato didn't consider while walking through the forementioned olive groves.

•

The cave – I did get there – was actually well worth the walk. It was huge. Well, I don't know if it was *huge*, but it was big enough for the batmobile. That came to mind because there was a bat, a rather fat bat, doing its bat thing up amidst all the incredible rock icicle things (I can never remember whether they're the stalactites or the stalagmites, so I call them rock icicle things). I'd never seen anything like it. The cave, I mean.

Though I'd never seen a fat bat before either.

Too Stupid to Visit

I've seen a cute little baby bat that was hibernating one winter tucked all cozy, dry and snug, between the plastic I'd put over my windows and the wood siding. And I've seen an injured bat that tore its wing – I tried to fix it with scotch tape. (That didn't work, by the way.) But I've never seen a fat bat before. And there it was fluttering around and occasionally hanging upside down on one of those rock icicle things.

•

On the way back from the cave, I saw some trees, evergreens of some kind, that were oddly cone-shaped, rising straight up out of the ground. Rather like, now that I think of it, copycat stalagmites – the opposite of rock icicles. Which is interesting, because the trees wouldn't've ever *seen* the stalagmites.

•

I also saw a sign outside a small Greek hotel named Virgina. The sign said, "Virgina – Vacantly."

•

You know, when you walk, you see a lot more than when you drive. A little later, I saw a rat. I'd never actually seen a rat before. Mice yes – cute little Mickey Mouse deer mice, and the other kind with the brown fur. But not a rat. Well, there was the white rat we were supposed to dissect in science class, but that wasn't a real out and about *rat* rat.

'Course, this one wasn't really out and about either. Well It was out, but since it was dead, it wasn't really about …

•

When I finally got back to my hotel, I figured a swim would be nice. People should really be more careful about how they use words. When I asked where the nearest beach was, I was directed to a stretch of water with rocks. They call it a "pebble beach". I call it a shoreline.

So when I asked the next person, I specified *sandy* beach. Though that wasn't likely to be any better, since the famous "black sand" beach on Santorini wasn't sand, it was grit.

And just for the record, it was more grey than black.

•

Florence is rather like Paris in its attitude toward pedestrians, because in Italy there are no sidewalks at all.

Well, there *are* – but apparently they're for the cars.

•

Another interesting thing about Italy is that the street people don't ask you for money exactly – they pray for it. Literally: they kneel on the sidewalk with their little cup in front of them and pray, hands pressed together, eyes closed, the whole bit.

Which has a weird effect. It makes you feel guilty if you don't give: how can we call ourselves Christians if we don't give to the poor? But then as soon as you do give, well, the person's prayers are answered, thanks be to – wait a minute! That was *me* who put the dollar in your cup, not God! Thanks be to *me!* (I'm God!)

•

While I was sitting in a restaurant, I saw a waiter take three dead fish on a plate to some people at one of his tables, I guess so they could choose which one they wanted. At first I thought, 'Ugh!' But then I thought, 'Well, people choose which lobster they want from a bunch swimming around in a tank.'

So okay, let's at least be consistent then. Next time someone orders wiener schnitzel, let's bring out all the little baby calves to frolic around the table.

('Course if they're gonna be veal, they've been kept too weak to frolic …)

Too Stupid to Visit

·

In Vienna, I went to see a Wagner opera, "The Ring Cycle", at the famous – and beautiful, lush, with red velvet everywhere ... – Staatsoper. My standing room spot was in the second side balcony. On my way up, and up, I had to stop for a nosebleed.

Then as I continued, I noticed a lot of fire extinguishers on the way. And I thought, 'Of course: a fire here would be a *big* problem.' A little later, a little higher, it occurred to me that what I saw could have been oxygen tanks.

The view from the stage must've been magnificent. The view from where I was, however – well, you could only see part of the stage. Unless you leaned out, over the balcony. Which was what the guy in front of me kept doing. Just as I was about to say, "Sir, would you please sit down, don't do that, you're making me nervous," I was distracted by the brass section (we had a great view of the orchestra pit): the horn players were placing bets with each other – I didn't know on what, I just figured okay, I'm not the only one who's bored with Wagner after five minutes. Then suddenly the guy in front of me *did* lean out too far. He went over, down I don't know how many hundred feet, and half the horn section let out a cheer.

I think I was especially bored because I didn't know what was going on. Because of the horn players, I missed the English translation on the little screen about the ring thing – what the ring was all about. I did catch the bit about Brünnhilde, whose horse, Grane, who she was giving to Siegfried, had lost all its strength when she rode it. Well, she's a big woman. I have nothing against big women, but there are some things large people shouldn't do and ride horses is probably one of them.

After a while I gave up my spot at the railing and sat on the floor and the next thing I knew Siegfried was giving Grane to someone else –

poor horse, kept being given away. And when asked if he took anything from the treasure he'd found, Siegfried says – well he sings of course – "Only this scrap of net, it's not worth much, you can have it." And the other guy sings back, "Oh that's Nibelung's work, it's magic, when you wear it, you can change shape." And Siegried sings back, "Oh don't I feel stupid."

Then I noticed the two harp players – both women – behind the horn section. As soon as their bit in the overture was done, they took off for a cup of tea and came back in an hour or so – in good spirits apparently – (hm … maybe it wasn't tea then) – because they proceeded to provide visual commentary to the opera. "I have lost my way," one guy sang, and the first harp player put her hands to her cheeks, "Oh no!" And when the old guy said to Siegfried, "Take this" – I don't know what it was, a horse maybe, probably Grane – "and you can have the woman too," they both gave him the finger.

•

And that was the end of my trip to Europe. Next day, I flew home from the Vienna airport. Where they have a drug-sniffing dog. I'd never seen one of those before. This one was really happy doing its job. Every time it completed a circuit of the passenger waiting room, it got a red ball to play with. Yippee!!

I think we all should get a red ball to play with when we've done our jobs.

Other Funny Bits

I was sitting in a restaurant one day and there was a family of four at the next table, the kids getting impatient. So the mother stopped the waitress and asked if she could bring the kids' dinners now.

The waitress replied, "They're not ready yet."

The mother said, "You mean you actually have to cook the hamburgers?"

"Ma'am, we actually have to sledgehammer the cow, drain its blood, scrape out its guts, and chop up what's left.

"Did you want fries with that?"

•

How a Dog is Not Like a Kid

1. A dog is generally kept on a leash when in public.

2. When a kid gets tired in public, it whines and tugs and whines – instead of quietly curling up and falling asleep at your feet.

3. A dog can be toilet-trained in a week or two.

4. A dog doesn't bark nearly as much as a kid cries, screams, wails, and shrieks. And it will seldom wake up in the middle of the night for just that very purpose.

5. A dog sits on command. And comes when you call.

6. A dog usually gets spayed and neutered before it reaches puberty.

7. A dog's destructive period generally lasts about a year. Not ten. (Thirty, in the case of males.)

8. And yet hotels, motels, apartments, and condos are far more likely to have a "No Dogs" rule than a "No Kids" rule. (And those that allow kids don't have a weight limit.)

•

I think they should design veterinary clinics to look like cars. Replace the front door with something off an old Chevy, put car seats in the waiting room, and put a huge fan in the corner going at 50 miles an hour. Dogs'd *love* going to the vet!

•

I once saw three big fish in a teeny little front yard pond.

Must've taken a whole two seconds for Bob to swim from one end to the other, passing Harry and then Joe on the way there, and again on the way back.

I sure hope all three have that short-term memory thing where you can't remember what you just did.

•

Ever see two snails chasing each other?

•

An American told me that they'd considered taking certain action against Canada, as revenge for not supporting them in one of their wars. "But," he explained, they decided not to because – "we sort of consider Canada our little brother, you know?"

Revenge for not supporting them? Who's the little brother?

"We protect you," he continued, seeing expression on my face. "You benefit from our defence."

Yeah, right. Like the safest place to be is right beside the jerk who's mouthing off and waving a big gun. Right beside the asshole everyone wants to just sit down and shut the fuck up.

And by the way, if you're so proud to be American, why do you wear a Canadian flag when you travel?

•

Too Stupid to Visit

George Carlin with Tourette's Syndrome: "Republican! Priest!"

·

Isn't it amazing what biological research is doing for agriculture? We have nectarines – a peach without the fuzz. And seedless grapes – that must have been a trick. And now boneless chicken.

Wouldn't that make life in the barnyard a little difficult?

·

Billboards can be great fun. I saw this ad on a board once: "Motorcycle for sale, 1993 Nighthawk, excellent condition, ridden only once."

And below it, in the same handwriting: "Wanted – wheelchair."

·

And this one: "Dog, free to a good home, one year old, mixed breed, curious and clever, playful disposition, not good for poultry farm."

Especially if it's a poultry farm for those new boneless chickens.

·

Commercials can be fun too. Remember there was one, it didn't get aired for very long, there's this couple in bed, he's already rolled over and sound asleep, she's sitting up with a look of – well – disappointment, but there's a bunch of other stuff there too, you know the look ...

Anyway, it was an ad for a pregnancy test: "It takes less time than he did."

·

Why is Aunt Jemima a maid and Uncle Ben a chef?

And *Mr.* Clean – yeah right.

·

The other day, I was walking along the street and I saw these guys, city maintenance workers – you know, with the grimy overalls and hard hats ...

Anyway, I see *seven* of them all standing around this sewer hole. So I stopped. I mean, this was a remarkable sight. They'd taken off the cover and were all standing around, looking down at it, and talking in those voices normally reserved for football and tires ...

And I thought, 'How many men does it *take* to clean a sewer?'

Then I thought, 'A lot more than seven since I've heard one can't even clean a diaper.'

•

Heard an ad for a car the other day talking about its 'advanced anti-impact system'. What is that, a fender?

•

Have you seen that show "Dogs with Jobs"?

I've got a companion show to pitch. "Cats on Unemployment."

•

Speaking of which, they say curiosity killed the cat.

Maybe the first eight times.

The ninth time? That had to've been stupidity.

•

Several studies have found that 50% of the male population approves of using force to get sex.

And the product advertised to make women feel safe is a fucking napkin.

•

Too Stupid to Visit

You know what women like about their periods? They're regular. They're every 28 days, give or take.

Wouldn't it be nice if *men* knew when they were being taken over by their chemicals?

•

For the record, I don't become bitchy for a few days a month.

I develop a heightened sensitivity to other people's many flaws.

•

Men lie to get sex. I've never had to. Not one man has ever said 'no'.

Men are such sluts, aren't they?

•

In our society, girls still get the impression that men as a whole are better than women. After all, they're the presidents and the CEOs and even the supervisors.

But when you raise a girl to believe that all men are better than her, you raise her to date, have sex with, fall in love with, and marry any old asshole. Because even he knows more, can do more, can do better –

Oh. That's *why* girls are still led to believe that men as a whole are better than women ...

•

Have you heard about William Lucas Barker?

The guy's been tested positive for the AIDS virus and he's threatened to 'take all the women with him that he can'. So far he's been charged with four counts of "Assault with a Deadly Weapon" – a neat twist on 'This is my penis, this is my gun', eh?

Anyway, what I'm wondering is why isn't the charge first degree murder? It's an interesting legal question, isn't it? I mean, does the victim have to be dead before you charge someone with murder?

•

And there's a prostitute in Oakland who's also tested positive, and she's declared she's going to keep on working. She seems to have done Barker one better, because the police can't find any victims: "Honey, I have something to tell you, I'm dropping out of the race for mayor ..." The perfect crime.

•

Speaking of perpetual hard-ons, you know how they're always saying they can't control it?

Yeah right. They control 94% of the planet's property, 96% of its politics, and 98% of its money.

But they just *cannot* control their own penises.

•

I happened to go to a blood donor clinic at a military college one time, and these guys were passing out like dominoes, and I thought, 'What good is a soldier who faints at the sight of blood?'

Actually, the nurse explained, it's a psychological contagion effect – apparently it's very common: one does it, they all do it.

Well that's different. That we *do* need in a soldier.

•

I'd like to comment, though, on the hysterical fear a lot of soldiers have of gays: how can they face the enemy if they can't even face homosexuality?

•

Too Stupid to Visit

Have you heard they used radioactive bullets in the Gulf War? Yeah, they finally figured out what to do with all that nuclear waste.

I guess when you get hit, you glow in the dark. I mean your hair probably falls out and your insides probably melt down but hey, you get a good glow.

So much for that brand new camouflage outfit.

•

Did you know there's an international law that says you can't use weapons that cause "unnecessary suffering"?

Blowing off your right leg, that was necessary.

But the left leg, gee, sorry about that, that *was* unnecessary, wasn't it.

•

I like language to be precise. And one of the things I hate is redundancy.

Like the other day, I heard this woman say to some guy, "You are a sick man!"

•

Speaking of language, does anyone else like to do crosswords? I was working on an interesting crossword the other day, actually a bit of a weird one, let me try a few out on you:

What's another word for 'man' – last three letters are e-n-t.

'Accident'? Close – 'experiment'!

Oh don't be offended, no doubt 'man' is being used in the generic sense, it includes men *and* women, isn't that what you're always telling us?

•

Jass Richards

What's another word for 'unannounced nuclear test'?

'Accident'! There it is!

·

How do you turn a rainforest into a desert?

Eat a hamburger.

·

You know how every time there's a move to stop cutting down forests, there's a hue and cry from the guys who will have to find another job?

Lumberjacks are like bricklayers who saw the fallen Berlin Wall as an employment opportunity.

·

Most life forms change their environment in ways that enhance their lives. We're changing our environment in ways that ensure our death.

Which means either we're really really stupid.

Or really really smart.

·

So, should we fund a mission to Mars?

Sure. Give us a bit of time and we can make that planet uninhabitable too.

·

I read about a woman who escaped from Saudi Arabia; she's in hiding here because there's a warrant out for her arrest – if she returns, she could be killed or she may just be stoned, flogged, and beaten.

Nevertheless, the Canadian Minister of Immigration won't let her stay because there are "no humanitarian or compassionate grounds" that apply to her case.

Too Stupid to Visit

You have to wonder, is English this guy's first language?

•

Read about another woman who had her hands uncovered, and the authorities threatened her with an "inspection of virginity".

Where did these guys get their sex ed from?

•

Each year a hundred men kill their female partners, but only three women kill their male partners.

So I'm thinking there's a real opportunity for assertiveness training seminars.

•

This male friend of mine was encouraging me to go bungee jumping, rock climbing, white water rapidding – whatever – "Women need to have more risk-taking in their lives," he said.

"Hell," I told him, "a lot of us are still going out with men, isn't that enough?"

•

Got a donation request the other day from the Alzheimers' Society. And I was actually gonna write out a cheque.

But then I – forgot.

•

HIgh school sucked, didn't it.

And those were the *best* years of our lives.

•

I ran track in high school. I never won or anything, but I was consistently at the front of the chase pack for the hundred metres.

•

Had a mastectomy the other day.

I thought, 'Cool, now I can get the sex change operation at a discount.'

•

What's black and blue?

A sad African-American.

•

What's white and blue?

A hospital sign.

•

Dontcha hate shopping? I was shopping for a tombstone the other day – well, I'm not gonna feel like it when I'm dead, am I!

•

Ever notice how stuff for women is more expensive than the same stuff for men? Clothes. Car repairs. Have you heard of those new female condoms? $8.00 for a box of three. That's about four times the price of male condoms. They're called "Reality Condoms". At least they got the name right.

•

Been to an art gallery lately? Last time I went, I thought, 'Hey, I can do that. I'll paint a wall grey and call it "Flock of Pigeons in the Fog – Contemplating Existentialism".'

•

Too Stupid to Visit

I was reading about cave art, at one of the displays, about how there are a lot more pictures of animals drawn in profile than in frontal view. Apparently because the frontal view is a sophisticated perspective requiring cognitive skills present only in more evolved brains.

There's a simpler explanation. The guys who actually saw a woolly mammoth head-on? They died.

•

I guess baseball's become America's favourite sport.

Seems everyone's carrying a baseball bat these days.

•

I'm thinking of getting a small handgun – y'know, just to keep in the house.

That way, when the burglar breaks in for my stereo, he'll have something to shoot me with.

•

People make a lot of assumptions about Canada. For example, a lot of people assume that Canada Post is a postal system. This is simply not true. It's an Examination Centre for Orienteering 101.

People also assume that we all live in igloos. And that's not true either. As in the U.S., a significant number of us live in parks, abandoned cars, and refrigerator boxes.

And people think Canada is pure and clean – you know, the Great White North. Yeah right. We've got so much toxic waste, tailings alone could stretch along the entire TransCanada highway and make a pile six feet high. We don't know what to do with the stuff – but we keep making it.

Jass Richards

And Canadians are supposedly a peace-loving people. Uh-huh. That's why we spent more on one Heavy Logistics Wheeled Military Vehicle than was in our entire Disarmament Fund.

•

Jack and Jill went up the hill
To fetch a pail of water
Jack fell down and broke his crown
And Jill said, "Clumsy!"

•

Men who think bigger is better are usually – fat.

•

Leafblowers. Don't they make an awful noise? It's such an irritating whine. You know why, dontcha? Because they were made for men – by men.

And the damn things don't even really clean up the leaves, they just move the mess from one place to another. So typical. Can you imagine if we designed vacuum cleaners that way?

•

White men are so stupid. They even got the national anthem wrong. It should've been "O Canada, our home *on* native land."

•

Bought a birthday present for my nephew the other day.

Why is it that toy guns are okay, but toy thumbscrews are considered sick?

•

If orgasms relax you, why are men so fucking uptight and hostile all the time?

Too Stupid to Visit

Either they're not getting as much as they say they are or they're faking it.

•

It's always pissed me off how men seem to make every little thing they do *so* important. They put on *such* a serious face. Even if they're just tying their shoelaces.

Turns out I've been giving them way too much credit. They're not conveying importance. They're just concentrating really really hard.

•

Someone once told me that the virus is the only life form that requires a higher life form in order to replicate.

Um, men.

•

"Y'know why women can't play poker?" this guy asked me once. "'Cuz they're no good at bluffing."

Well, I guess you've never had sex with a woman then, eh?

•

I read the other day about a new proposed crime, "Negligent Rape", in which a man *fails to notice* a woman's lack of consent.

Guys. How can you fail to notice "GET THE FUCK OFF ME!"?

•

Wouldn't it be nice if women had voluntary control over ovulation?

Wouldn't it be even better if men had voluntary control over ejaculation.

Oh wait –   They pretty much do.

Jass Richards

•

At every age over fifteen, more women than men receive treatment for mental health problems. Scarey, eh? All those men walking around out there ... untreated.

•

Research continues to show that the older you get, the less likely you are to get married.

Well yeah. Because the older you get, the smaller your capacity for delusion.

•

You know he's a keeper when ...

His mama told him not to come. (And he has a pet bullfrog.)

He says that if you can't be with the one you love, you should love the one you're with.

He says he's gonna be with you tonight instead of all the whores on 8th avenue.

'Sorry' seems to be the hardest word.

He thinks you're having his [sic] baby to show how much you love him.

He shot someone. (The sheriff.) (But not the deputy, note.)

Indiana wants him.

You can tell by the way he uses his walk that he's a woman's man.

He says he's been through the desert. On a horse. With no name.

He has sex with a sixteen-year-old. Who has lips like strawberry cream.

Too Stupid to Visit

He says things like "Someone left the cake out in the rain, I don't think that I can take it, 'cause it took so long to bake it, and I'll never have that recipe again. Oh no."

•

Ya gotta love automated answering systems: Press 1 for sales, 2 for service, and 3 if you have *no* short-term memory whatsoever.

•

Hello, this is Dial-a-Psychic. How can I help you?

Don't you know?

•

According to Manly Palmer Hall, "We are all healthy when we are not thinking about ourselves."

Speak for yourself. I'm not such a basket case that I can't bear the thought of me.

•

How many philosophers does it take to change a light bulb?

Define 'light bulb'.

•

Have you seen those extra large chocolate bars with the re-sealable packages?

Why would you need a re-sealable package on a chocolate bar?

•

I love it when wrongs get righted, and justice prevails. For example, all those companies putting CFCs into the atmosphere, wrecking the ozone, and giving us all skin cancer?

Jass Richards

Wouldn't it be cool if they were all owned by rich black people?

·

What's with the rule that only big motherfuckers can be firefighters?

Are they trying to make *sure* the burning buildings collapse under their weight?

Or only when they're carrying an extra hundred pounds of rescued kid?

·

I came across an interesting proposal the other day: what if people who wanted to create a new human being had to get a license to do so?

The creation of old human beings wasn't considered.

·

Studies show that people with mentors advance in their careers more than those without mentors.

See, I've never had a mentor.

'Course, I've never had a career.

·

For a while – a short while – I was a high school teacher.

A little known Murphy's Law states that in every class there shall be at least one student with a multiple personality disorder.

When you take attendance, this student will answer "Here!" to *every* name that's called.

You will therefore have to pass a sheet of paper around the room for signatures.

Too Stupid to Visit

It will be necessary, however, to escort the sheet of paper because otherwise the students will sign each other's names.

Except for those with delusions of grandeur who will sign, simply, "God".

I did make it clear to those chosen few that they were not God.

I was.

Escorting the paper around the room will take at least ten minutes because half of the students will not have a pen or pencil with which to *write* their names and half will not *know* their names.

Unfortunately, it's never the same half.

I solved the problem one day by taking a snapshot of the class.

Word got out, however, and the next time I tried that, I ended up with a very nice photograph of 27 bare asses. None of which I could identify.

Shortly after this Kodak moment, I found myself in the principal's office. Again.

He had in his hand one of my writing assignment topics: 101 things to do with your Barbie doll.

He said that he was getting a lot of negative reports about me which he found disturbing.

So, I told him, don't read them.

By the way, how many students does it take to change a light bulb?

"That's the janitor's job, let him do it, he's getting paid."

Allow me to present a character sketch of Willy the Wasteland, the class rep.

First and foremost, Willy the Wasteland is bored.

He is especially and chronically bored in class because he can't change channels.

He has to watch the same program for a whole hour.

It has only one set.

There is no soundtrack.

There is a sound effect though – a bell.

It makes Willy salivate.

The camera uses only one angle. Unless you get up out of your seat and move around a lot. Which Willy does. A lot.

And the program happens in real time: in one hour, only one hour passes by.

This state of affairs is a problem for Willy because he can't concentrate under these conditions.

'Course it is my belief he may not be able to concentrate under *any* conditions.

Because, you see, on the radio, there's a different song every 3 minutes and in between, a different combination of voices every 30 seconds advertising a different product. The DJ changes pitch more often in one sentence than most of us do in a whole day.

And in the newspaper – should Willy be able to read – material is presented in bits and pieces seldom longer than two or three hundred words with individual sentences of only seven or eight words.

Music videos are similarly fragmented into a visual strobe. So unless it moves, Willy just can't see it.

It is my belief that Willy is evolving into a frog.

•

Too Stupid to Visit

How I Spent My Summer Vacation

Upon hearing that the gravel pit out my way was going to be in operation 24/6, for two years, I decided it was time for a change. After some exciting competition, I was offered a position as a Test Specialist with the people who create the LSAT. (Who says a Philosophy degree is useless?) I accepted, and Chessie and I (Chessie's the canine I live with) packed up half of our stuff into a U-Haul truck and headed to Newtown, PA. The following 'Things to Know' and 'Things to Expect' might be of interest to those considering a similar move.

#1 - Be very nice to the border guard whose decision it will be whether or not you get a work visa. When he questions you about the degree you show him and asks you to get your transcripts, do not object. (If I'd known they would be in the last box I looked in, I would've looked in that one first.)

#2 - In most parking lots, you will have only an inch clearance on both sides when you park and unpark your U-Haul. You will therefore ding (okay, lift and sort of drag away) some guy's fender. (You will also give new meaning to the phrase 'a drive-through'.)

#3 - Have ready lots of American coinage; holding up traffic at a toll booth offering to barter your Logic 101 textbook will not go over well.

#4 - Because of the visual peculiarities of a U-Haul (i.e., you can't see a damned thing behind you), changing lanes will take longer than usual. (The strategy I developed was to put my blinker on for a full minute, to give everyone time to get out of the way, and then just move over.) (It seemed to work quite well.) You will therefore miss at least one exit. It will be the one to bypass a major city. The major city you will then pass through will be experiencing rush hour at the time. It will also be experiencing extensive roadwork, involving extensive detours.

#5 - Your actual time of arrival will be significantly different than your expected time of arrival. The key word here is 'significantly' – despite having made reservations, you will be unable to check-in.

#6 - Sleeping in the front seat of a U-Haul with your dog will not be as uncomfortable as you might think.

#7 - The homefinder service you hired will not find you a home. They will merely fax you listings.

#8 - The motel you're staying at will not have a fax machine.

#9 - The nearby (sort of) print shop will. But it will not accept a travellers' cheque unless it's for the exact amount (it seems they can't make change; and silly me, I didn't get a traveller's cheque in the amount of $6.42).

#10 - You will have to go apartment-hunting in your U-Haul. There is no public transit in the Newtown area. And you can't lease a car without a PA driver's licence, you can't get a PA driver's licence without a social security card, and you can't get a social security card until you have a fixed address. And you can't even rent a car for a few days unless you have a fixed address and a social security number; one agency would've rented with my Ontario driver's licence and proof of Ontario car insurance, but, when I sold my car back home, I cancelled my auto insurance. (What was I thinking?)

#11 - You will pay around $650/month for a one-bedroom apartment. Plus utilities. Plus grass-cutting. Plus garbage pick-up. Plus appliance maintenance and repair.

#12 - Did I say 'plus utilities'? You can't get your utilities turned on until you have a social security number.

#13 - At the social security office, you will have to take a number and wait. Since there will be only one counter person, for a standing room only situation, take a book. But not that Logic 101 textbook.

Too Stupid to Visit

#14 - Getting from the U-Haul depot to your new apartment will be nothing short of miraculous. Not only is there no public transit, there are no taxis. (Staring in disbelief at the Ts in the yellow pages, you will vaguely wonder if a taxidermist wouldn't be of value right about now.) Don't underestimate, however, the kindness of strangers (well, that and the power of the image of a poor little blind dog left all alone in a strange apartment full of boxes anxiously waiting for you to come back).

#15 - The difference between a mild case of poison ivy and a severe case of poison ivy can be as little as eight hours. (I spent Sunday wondering how I could be Chessie's seeing eye person if my other eye swelled shut.) (And as I prepared Monday morning for my first day on the job, blistered and oozing with pus, I decided that yes, one can make a fashion statement with strips of gauze.)

Three weeks later (still no social security card) (but that's okay – still no car lease) (but that's okay – still no car insurance), I get news from back home: it seems the contractor for the highway expansion has found another gravel pit to use.

#16 - Though one can rent a U-Haul one way from North Bay to Newtown, one cannot rent a U-Haul one way from Newtown to North Bay; however ...

•

So while I was looking for a new job, everyone kept saying "You're overqualified."

Yeah, well, the jobs I'm qualified for are filled.

By men.

Saw an ad for a food demonstrator.

"Ladies and gentlemen, may I have your attention please? This – is food."

•

Saw an ad for a bingo caller and I thought, 'Hey, I can do that! I've got my Sesame Street Graduation Diploma!' But the ad said, "Experience Required".

What's to require experience? B-5.

•

I was a lumber grader. For a day.

Apparently when you grade lumber, you take *off* marks for originality.

(Slabs of wood in a warehouse, kids in a classroom, who knew there was a difference?)

•

Saw an ad for a poet for a greeting card company. Even submitted a portfolio.

"You light up my life. / Like an oncoming train."

"I'm sorry we fought last night. / I'm much more vicious during the day."

"Heard you were ill, injured, whatever – / Can I borrow your car this weekend?"

•

Too Stupid to Visit

One place had a really long application form. Desperate, I answered every question.

Previous Place of Employment: The company that employed me was called Drake Overload.

Employee Name: Jass Richards

Location: I have no recollection of the actual location I was dispatched to. I don't remember where it was, how I got there, or what the building looked like. I can remember only the small room I was put in. I'm told that that's common for torture victims.

When, and for How Long, Did You Work at This Job? Until lunch.

What Was Your Job Title? Office Temp

What Was Your Real Job Title? Address-Label Sticker-onto-Envelopeser

How Long Did It Take Before You Started Looking for a New Job? Never stopped.

How Much Money Did You Make at This Job? Minimum wage. Duh.

How Did You Get Back-and-Forth to This Job? Apparently I passed through a time-space portal into another world. Another life with another me. Because the real me would never have been in that position.

What Was Your Commute Time To This Job? I have no recollection. None whatsoever.

Jass Richards

What Was The Physical Environment Like at This Job? It was a small room. The walls were beige. There was a table. It was a large table, like the kind in school cafeterias. There was one chair. It was a wooden chair. I vaguely remember shackles on the legs, but that could have been my imagination. On the table were boxes. And boxes. And boxes. Some contained reams (and reams) of sheets on which there were self-sticking address labels. Ten to a sheet. Other boxes contained envelopes. The white office-letter ones.

What Was The Emotional Environment Like at This Job? At the beginning, I felt challenged. To endure. That lasted a full minute.

Did You Have Any Nemeses at This Job? The woman, I don't remember her name, who led me into the room and indicated that I was to sit in the chair at the table. She explained what would happen. Then left. A couple hours later, she returned, glanced at the situation, and told me I wasn't going fast enough. Despite my having the manual dexterity of an accomplished pianist. "Not *quickly* enough," I corrected her. Because I have an English degree.

Did You Have Any Allies at This Job? No. I saw no one else while I was there. I heard screams though.

What Was/Were Your Living Situation(s) Like While You Were Working Here? I can't recall. I must have been living somewhere though because I needed rent money.

When Did You Know That You Didn't Want This Job Anymore? When I saw the advertisement.

What Was Your Departure Like From This Job? An intriguing mix of humiliation and joy.

Too Stupid to Visit

What Do You Think About When You Think About This Job? In all these years since, I haven't actually thought about it until now. Thanks a lot.

•

I eventually got a job in a half-way housing program run by the mental health association, helping the residents transition from institutionalized living to independent living.

Since I mostly covered the midnight shift, that meant I helped them make the transition from sleeping in a bed to sleeping in a bed.

And I was really good!

But I have to say, people who need people are – codependent.

While I was there, I tried running a support group for people in denial. But no one ever came.

Even so, I kept my sense of humour.

Why did the passive personality cross the road?
Because I told him to.

Why did the multiple personality cross the road?
Are you asking *me*?

Why did the paranoid person cross the road?
Why do you ask?

Why did the delusional person cross the road?
Because he thought the grass was greener on the other side.

Why did the masochist cross the road?
He didn't. Because the grass *was* greener.

Why did the hallucinating person cross the road?
To follow the boneless chicken.

www.ingramcontent.com/pod-product-compliance
Lightning Source LLC
Chambersburg PA
CBHW030157100526
44592CB00009B/327